Emma's Little Book of Poetry

AF632817

Emma Valerie Rose

BookLeaf Publishing

Presentation by *BookLeaf Publishing*

Web: www.bookleafpub.com

E-mail: info@bookleafpub.com

ISBN: 9789357211178

First edition 2022

DEDICATION

In loving memory of Josh, Jessica, Grandad Dave, Grandad Tony, Grandad Vic, Nan Mandy, Uncle Scott, Uncle Pete and Edna.

ACKNOWLEDGEMENT

for Mom, Dad, Gary, Nan Rose, Auntie Maz, Abbie, Auntie Carole, Chrisy, Uncle Mark and Auntie Elaine, Uncle Darren and Auntie Paulette, Sophie, Hughie, Mr Strachan, Gregory Leadbetter and Derek Littlewood.

Surrounding Me

You've been gone for years
but it feels like a century.
Five years fraught with fear,
none of us able to see a world without you here.

We miss your laugh that bubbled through the air,
the way you squinted through your glasses,
your playful scolding of the cat.
We learned that hot July day that life isn't fair,
and with every year that passes
we're still learning to accept that.

Even though you're gone,
I can feel you surrounding me.
You're here to reassure, not to haunt
and I can hear your voice in my ear saying,
"Stop your blarting" -
so I don't lose my way in this mourning.

Gingerbread Whiskers

Gingerbread whiskers,
Gumdrop smile
with a hint of whiskey.
Caramel eyes
with a hint of cocoa.

Traces of gunmetal against
soft auburn hair failed to
betray your age,
or accentuate
the gathered skin around your eyes.

Gingerbread whiskers
and a gumdrop smile
drowning in whiskey.

Caramel eyes now
see only in sepia.

Aculeate

Burning, aching, raw
barbed edges sit under inflamed skin,
yet it still wants more,
setting me alight from within.

I remove the stinger with tremoring hands,
Grit my teeth against the pain,
Douse with water like my skin demands,
my body no longer its domain.

The worst is behind me,
just a small nick left behind
as a reminder of its stinging spree,
maybe by now, he'll have retired.

Parkrun

Our congregation gathers
at the start line,
huddling together against the elements.
Rain, snow, monsoon -
it doesn't matter, we'll run together.

Here we are all equal,
not a single drama
or argument to see here.
If you fall
we'll pick you back up,
and maybe after we'll
go for a beer.

Three. Two. One.

Off we go,
pounding the pavement -
cheers resonate around us,
echoing in the air.

Now all is said and done,
who's to say we can't have more fun?
Tea and cake at the Shed,
every human (and dog) well-fed.

Everyone here has won
after another successful Chasewater Parkrun.

Don't Lose Hope When You Need it Most

In the midnight hour
my eyes started to close,
when I heard a voice in my ear full of power,
"Don't lose hope when you need it most."

I closed my eyes,
and counted to ten,
waited at the precipice to watch yesterday die,
when I heard it again.

"Don't lose hope when you need it most" -
I didn't know there was hope to lose.

Sleep long abandoned, I got out of bed
and crossed over to the window,
the glass frigid against my head,
as I mourned the loss of my pillow.

On the window sill were fractured shards of
glass,
strewn along the plastic.
I waited there for the last of my hope to collapse
but my brain, ever the semantic,
fixated on the sun rising in the west.

A universal symbol of optimism and hope,
it made me question my inability to cope
with the inconsequential worries and fears,
that escaped my brain through the tears
that never seemed to cease.

I stayed at the window until the darkness faded,
until my fears were translated
into shadowy afterthoughts,
until the daily battles became uncommon
assaults.

Don't lose hope when you need it most.

Broken Poetry

My words don't rhyme,
my rhythm is non-existent,
my tone is too solemn -
tell me something I don't already know.

I write from the heart,
always have done,
and still will even though I've been caught
trying to extract too much meaning from the sun.
(There's some half-rhyme for you).

You call it broken poetry,
I call it perfect.
You call it dark and macabre -
well, I have to agree with you there.

Broken poetry might be the next big thing,
you don't want to miss it, darling.

Rolling with the Punches

We used to think we were cursed,
that the family name carried danger
and brought only pain.
"The Poynton curse", we affectionately named
it,
it's part of this crazy clan after all.

We've been through it all as a family -
injuries, betrayals, deaths and everything in
between.
You'd expect us to have been driven to insanity
but it's just part of our routine.

We're just rolling with the punches,
making the best out of bad situations.
Even when hope is snatched from our clutches,
we continue to dash expectations
as we keep rolling with the punches.

Love Me, Don't Leave Me

That effervescent smile masks broken eyes,
your once rosy cheeks sunken and pale.
These silent screams are deafening,
as I beg you to stay,
begging you to fight for us.

Love me, don't leave me,
I won't survive another heartbreak.
There's so much you can't see,
so much at stake.

Just say it.

Love me, don't leave me
alone, here, in the ruins of us.
You say you're happy
but -

Oh. I understand.

Love me or leave me,
It's okay, you can go.
Let me make your decision easy,
No one else will ever know.

You're in My Past Now

The ghost of your kiss lingers on my lips,
your embrace just a fading memory.
I wish I knew it wouldn't be a quick fix,
because now you've got me begging for a
remedy.

It feels as though you've ripped my heart out
and trampled all over it,
making me doubt, and doubt, and doubt
everything I ever dared to admit.

You're in my past now,
Your lies can't hurt me anymore.
Still the same tricks, like a predator on the
prowl,
waiting for your next score.

I will pick myself back up and find myself
in the midst of all this confusion.
No, I don't need your help -
I just need this chapter to reach its conclusion.

Reflection

Years ago, I couldn't look in the mirror -
those eyes were glassy, full to bursting
with unshed tears from school days,
skin speckled with spots sore to touch,
lips bitten to the verge of blood.

Then I found her.

Like twins separated at birth,
we came together by some twist of fate.
Just a stone's throw away,
our lives collided.
Parents with the same names,
one party cruel and the other kind,
brothers who knew each other
from days of playing football on the fields.

When does that ever happen?

She taught me what it is to be happy,
how it feels to be appreciated.
My best friend, my soul sister,
she pulled me out of the darkest places.

One day I finally returned to the looking glass.

Who was this?

Cerulean eyes full of hope, joy and promise,
skin speckled with beauty marks,
rosebud lips stretched in a smile.
I love this version of me,
and it's because of her
that I can look at my reflection again.

Cat at the Bottom of my Garden

I saw her at the bottom of my garden,
lying stock still against the gravel.
She looked to be asleep from the safety of my window,
but up close I learned the full story.

Paws frozen in the air
as I manoeuvred her gently,
her chest unmoving,
rigid body cold to the touch
despite the searing heat in the air.

Around her neck was a collar without a name,
without a clue of who she was to somebody.
Her fur gave way to the delicate probing touch of my fingers,
as I searched for her identity -
Surely someone out there is missing her?

She continues to reside in my garden
covered by a blanket against the gravel,
until someone decides to claim her
and give her the goodbye she deserves.

Silence is Looming over Us

The silence looms over us
the longer we keep going
on this self-destructive path.

"Hide your pain, conceal your feelings,
they don't matter."

The silence will loom over us
every day until we take a stand
and prove it wrong,
proving that our feelings are important,
until we can make everyone feel heard.

"Don't hide your pain, share the burden."

Lend your neighbour a kind ear,
allow them to lift the weight off their chest
that heaves with unshed tears.

Don't let the silence win,
don't acknowledge its existence.

Don't let it loom over us any longer.

Under the Lights

Our community is condensed to just thirty
thousand tonight,
standing up from our seats as we wait for the
lights to go down.

Wolf heads surround us as the lights
start to die, giving way to music
with bass that vibrates through our chests.

"Want you to see all of the lights."

Golden strobing lights travel across the stadium,
illuminating each wanderer's face
as the time ticks down with every
strobing spotlight that passes us.

All at once, the music dies and the lights are
revived
as we, the roaring crowd, grow louder
waiting for our heroes to make their entrance
under the lights of our golden palace.

Look at Me Now

I know you've been trying to get in touch,
but I don't want to feel the same panic,
anxiety and confusion I felt every day at school.
For now, you're blocked from my life
and it'll stay that way for as long as possible.

Look at me now,
You told me I'd never amount to anything,
that I'd never make it anywhere,
that I'd never find anyone.
Well, that last part might be true
but I'm becoming someone I'm finally proud of.

I hope you're achieving what you want from life
and I mean that with the most sincerity,
but you've got to understand I won't talk to you
so I can keep my integrity.

I harbour no ill will towards you,
or anyone that took part in the daily torment and ridicule,
as I left all that behind the day I left school.

Look at me now,
I've amounted to a lot,

I've got onto my Masters course,
and as for the finding someone to love part -
well, that last part might be true
but I finally feel proud to be me.

Old Bookshop

In my village stands the old bookshop,
between the butchers and bakery.
The old man working there serves the
community,
he's like a father to us all -

he invites us in with that mischievous smile
and comforts us with that sage-like
knowledge that comes so naturally to him -

until one day he wasn't there.

Illuminated only by the embers of those precious
books
stands a mere silhouette of what used to be -
years of whispered screams over coffee,
the comforting aroma of old paper hanging in
the air.

He'll try and rebuild, despite his better years
being far behind him,
saying he owes it to us and the memory of his
late wife,
whose memory remains alive in the pages
of his next chapter beyond

his old bookshop.

Work in Progress

Scattered ashes of the books she loved
and the lives we tried to build
are the only reminder of
what it meant to have normality.

I can still smell the thick smoke,
its plumes embedding themselves deep in my chest.
Still feels like I'm breathing through broken lungs,
but I suppose that will get better

soon, I'll revive her memory
in the words on the pages
of the book she never pursued.
"It's a work in progress", she used to tell me,
but she never got to see it through.

Even as I sit here in the ashes
of the shop we built together,
I know it'll all be okay,
that we'll survive.

This next chapter is a work in progress,
I've just got to trust the process.

Butterfly Kisses

Butterfly kisses,
the ghost of your arms wrapped around me.

There are days I miss it,
but then I remember there's nowhere else I want to be
than right here,

writing my poetry and living for my own means.

No More Emptiness

I'm not emotionless,
I have a heart that feels
and yearns and breaks
whenever I see that face.

What hurts the most is
there's nothing I can do
to heal or mend the emptiness.

If you think you can guilt me,
and invalidate my feelings,
and make me feel wrong,
you've got another thing coming
if you think you'll get me to hold my tongue.

You've overstayed your welcome
for over a year now.
Oh, dear Grief, you don't scare me anymore -

I may not be emotionless
but as the days and weeks tick by,
I can feel the emptiness
starting to subside.

Downing Street

Powerful speeches and poignant words
soon faltered off-camera,
after promising us the world
and we believed it.

Maybe he was still hungover
from the latest party at Downing Street?

He locked us away in our homes,
we served our house arrests dutifully
and missed out on vital moments
with family while he
partied and hollered
"hip hip hooray" at our expense.

The same old speeches,
and stagnant words fool no-one.
We should have known better
than to believe his broken promises.

It doesn't matter to him though -
even after the fines,
he's tucked safely away
at 10 Downing Street.

Hospital Poem

Onehundredandfifty

Ambulances race past me,
and I wonder which is mine.
My GP mentions sepsis,
clots, pulmonary embolisms -
okay, so maybe this is serious.

Onehundredandforty

Two hours later, I'm sat in a cubicle,
the blood pressure cuff pinching fine hairs on
my arm.
A needle punctures my skin until she finally
captures a vein,
but the fun isn't over yet,
the doctor wants an x-ray.

One hundred

Five hours into my unwanted excursion,
I'm sitting alone in a boiling-hot corridor,
the flickering lights above me doing nothing
to calm my racing heart.

I'm tired of this waiting,
tired and hungry -
hungry for answers, and in the literal sense.
The sandwich from earlier sits like a rock in my stomach,
the cheese like plastic and the ham
disconcertingly soft.

Ninety-nine.

Good news: my heart isn't about to explode,
Less good news: my asthma might be getting worse.

"Take care now."
The doctor's words are like music to my ears
as I hobble through the corridor
towards the exit.

I barely register the rest of the night
once I'm home,
instead I go to bed to stretch my aching limbs
and calm my poor heart.

Note to self: don't see that particular GP again.

Find Yourself

"Find yourself", screams the voice inside my
head,
but I thought I was already found.
I'm twenty, insecurity aplenty,
Tried to find my way forward,
found myself a million miles away instead.

My sexuality? Straight.
"No, you're lesbian."
Okay, I'm lesbian.
"No, you're bisexual."
Oh, okay.

I'm bisexual,
I know that now.
Girls, boys, girls, boys -
is this enough?

I'm starting to find myself
In a tidal wave of uncertainty.

www.ingramcontent.com/pod-product-compliance
Lightning Source LLC
Chambersburg PA
CBHW051754130826
49812CB00033B/1143
9789357211178